Eric Morrissey

Eric Morrissey was born in Cw
1948. He was educated at Aberdare Grammar School.
He joined the Royal Navy on May 6th, 1963, where he
continued his education at HMS Vincent, Gosport, and
HMS Collingwood, Portsmouth, where he qualified as an
electrical mechanic.

After leaving the Royal Navy he moved back to Aberdare,
before finally settling in Llechryd, with his wife, Sylvia.

He made two tours of the Far East where he enjoyed,
among other things, the oriental cultural differences
between Eastern and Western falconers. He became
fascinated with falconry and it was in the East where he
became interested in becoming an austringer: someone
who flies eagles and hawks as opposed to falcons.

Eric is also a keen naturalist and artist, using charcoals,
pastels, acrylic and oils. He used to be a dedicated
athlete, having raced in more than twenty marathons
(best time: 3hrs 12mins).

Tapestry of a Desert Nomad

Eric Morrissey

Parthian
The Old Surgery
Napier Street
Cardigan
SA43 1ED

www.parthianbooks.com

First published in 2013
© Eric Morrissey 2013
All Rights Reserved

ISBN 9781908946485

Cover by Eric Morrissey
Typeset by Elaine Sharples
Printed and bound by Dinefwr Press, Llandybie, Wales

Published with the financial support of the Welsh
Books Council.

British Library Cataloguing in Publication Data

A cataloguing record for this book is available from
the British Library.

A special thank you to Menna Elfyn, who has been a source of infinite patience, advice and inspiration. Thanks are also due to the following writing groups: Teifi Writers, Wings and not least, Scribes.

The Modern Coracleman won the Pembrokeshire Fish Week poetry prize.

Queen of the Valleys won first prize in the Trowell Open Poetry Competition.

Listed in alphabetical order are publications where some of my poetry first saw the light of day.
First Time
In The Country
Panda
Scribes
Teifi Whispers
My first collection, "Windows of the World Are Covered in Rain"

and

Wings

Foreword

The journey of a person writing poetry is never straightforward. In fact, it shouldn't be. It does require that act of travelling alone, through the dark, sensing fear and wonder in equal measure. Such is the journey of Eric Morrissey – for there are glimpses of that 'dark night of the soul' here, as well as the joy of morning, nature, and the pure delight of recognizing what it is to be alive:

Have the courage,
To cry,
In the shadow of a gelid sun

Many of these poems are crystalline particles of life that melt within. Others are 'wisps of sand'. But one thing is certain: that the voice within these poems impresses on the reader a sense of wonder at the world as well as a sense of vibrant urgency against its demise. These poems recall the rhythmic beat of the heart, the lost thoughts of the mind, reminding us that we are all mere nomads, possessing a rich tapestry woven as a gift from life, just as a poem is. As only a poem can be.

MENNA ELFYN

Contents

The Phurnacite, Abercwmboi

With tar laden brush-strokes; the chimney
washes the sky full of sulphured yellows,

and dark sooty shadows.

Staining the mountains with charred trees,
on acid stung grass;
colouring the valley with funereal flowers

after drawing in the acrid painted air,
to burn with deceitful, cancerous breaths;
slowly shading out the future.

Leaving leafless, fleshless skeletons,
of both plant and man;
stippling a dying countryside.

A caustic,
macabre masterpiece;
from the Coal Board's insidious palette.

Snake-bite

For days after the fangs
pierced my thumb
and glands pumped:

their venom.

I could taste the air, un-hinge my lower
jaw and swallow rabbits

whole.

I could twist my body into umpteen coils, unrolling
skin:

like a nylon stocking.

When the toxin eventually wore off, I stopped
hallucinating:

yet still spoke with a forked tongue.

Sea Snake

As it swam around me and before I knew how dangerous
it was, I stroked its chin, touched the top of its head.
Gently caressed it along the whole length of its muscular,
silk-rope-like-body. Tickled its belly and let it serpentine
through my loosely clenched hands.

Then the local pilot, who helped us navigate tricky
reefs, came running wildly, shouting hysterically in his
native tongue as he sprinted from the beach, splashing
through surf like a bear after salmon, only to grab this
beautiful animal by the tail and crack it like a whip –
so hard its head

flew off.

Headless, but still very much longer than my five-and-a-
half feet and still satin smooth to the touch, as I felt, when
I again ran my hands tenderly, from its quivering, ribboned
neck, all the way down to its dorsally flattened tail.

Yet each scale ripped off the skin, was hard as a sliver

of coral.

I could trace the striking black and silver pelt back to
land, where its spark of flint outshone church glass and
before its venom shattered the mirrored

gleam of ocean.

The Modern Coracleman

*Blue jean: The younger fishermen sometimes used scrap denim
from a local factory (which has since moved), in place of canvas
which in turn replaced hide.*

Splitting and knitting hazel bones;
into the skeleton of a shell-like ear
that wears blue jean over the weave.

Painted with perfect pitch;
it listens to the music of the river.

Seeing seven stars / seren saith,
he goes to work / mynd i'r gwaith.

Carved paddle placed over shoulder and prow,
feet braced at the square front corners;
he takes his net dancing to the tune of:

the Teifi.

Tapestry of a Desert Nomad

- *The lanner is an African falcon, smaller than a peregrine. It has a yellow-crowned head.*
- *Primaries – the main flight feathers.*
- *The barbaric practise of sewing eyelids shut as an aid to training is still sometimes used in the East. Western falconers make use of a leather hood.*

Wisps of sand rise in thermals of gritty flight
and the lanner's soft wings lay

on textured air.

She crests the rise, her sun coloured crown
flickering above our Bedouin camp and the freedom
of this nomadic tribe is pointedly described.

A falcon no longer bound by jess and leash.

Primaries slash scimitar scars into the shimmering
blue steel of a desert sky.

Eyes once sewn against the light, stitch-up her
intended first kill, pin sharp talons already pricked to
embroider prey;

with needle-point precision.

5

Llechryd After the Rain

Sewin: sea trout found in abundance in the river Teifi and a local delicacy preferred to salmon

The bridge is a riverbed.

Sewin swim the fields and cars drown
in lakes, as front doors open

onto waterfronts.

I think I'll swap my push-bike
for a coracle as the forecast warns sheep
to sleep in trees because next week we'll
again, be able to catch lobsters in

chimney pots.

Fathomless

A silver scaled song sung before dawn
of pebbles and rocks strummed
by the ebb and tone of tidal water

a king-fisher-blue anthem that rouses ring-ouzel
and yellow wagtail

as pulsing a rhythm of fish, the gurgle
of his voice glides across the valley floor.

The Teifi curls and stretches lazily
its classic water music touches your soul
with a tenor's summer lilt

before his winter baritone:

drowns fields and bridges.

Public Baths, Watford

For Roy

The utter luxury of soaking,
sitting bolt upright;
yet with shoulders submerged:

up to my neck in hot water:

but not the least sign of trouble.

Would-be Roust-a-Bout

A fairground away
your carousel of horses
stampeding.

Lightshade

This poem, out of a workshop by Paul Henry for Teifi Writers

The chandelier,
like satellite debris,
hanging in space,

dark stars,

lit in daylight
by the sun,
orbiting

the room.

Broken Glass

For Yvonne

In the mirror's brightest eye
seed was planted ripe to sprout
weed outgrew the crop of rye
a golden harvest:

lost to drought.

In the mirror's darkest gloom
death blossomed like a flower
the ripest head with deepest bloom
caught us in:

the nightmare hour.

In the mirror's faithless heart
lurked a black malevolent fist
one errant cell's malignant start
to a budding petal:

fatally kissed.

In the mirror's blind reflection
the rose garden turned to grass
a nightingale's rich music section
just splintered shards:

of broken glass.

Red Ash

For 'Ginger'

I was six or seven, my legs grew towards the ground from cuffs of scruffy shorts, my knees peeped over tops of wellies too big for veneer-thin-limbs that were grubby and grazed from too many tumbles on the small-coal-tip, where we had played all our young lives.

Our terraced homes backed onto a mountain stream that bubbled with trout and our fathers – all miners – built the railway-sleeper-bridge, over which the footpath ran beckoning us to;

"The Tip".

The warm smoking tip was less than fifty feet from my back-lane door.

Apart from the odd scrape or bruise, our coal-tip playground seemed safe and our parents always knew where we were, knew too, that a shout from a kitchen window would bring any of us scuttling home for tea.

Things were never the same after "Ginger" Rugman, racing back in response to his mother's call, broke through the small-coal-crust:

his wellies melted on his feet.

MS

For Kim, a team mate

Every touch,
a master stoke;
caressing the ball:

from tackle to pass.

Knitting,
plain with pearl;
weaving a magic tapestry:

of defence and attack.

Then,
That final season;

we thought you,
blasé;
couldn't be bothered:

that you no longer gave a toss.

We tied,
you down;
with insults.

Force-fed you profanity,

about your feet all thumbs.

We stitched you up,
and watched dumbfounded;
as you:

unravelled.

Heroin Heroine

Hypodermic eyes
needling away at
tomorrow's shroud.

Searching in vain,
for an un-collapsed vein
in your pathetic, punctured;

rapture ruptured: tortured body.

Care in the Community

In urban shadowlands,
at the grasping heart of
second millennium cities

boxed, in a clutter
of presentation packages,
the new netherclass flounder.

Discharged human wreckage
huddle in isolated cloisters,
hapless hunched bunches

of flotsam,
with fragile minds
wavering,

loitering,
in the chill wind
of desperation.

Sucking cold comfort
from
frosted bottles.

Dead wastelands
alive with spirits
killing old ghosts.

Communal sharps
dulled by disease
prick holes in their future.

The stench
of sweet dreams;

in a bitter ghetto.

Human Nature

Does it mean:

littering the road
with dead kittens,
flat hedgehogs
and putrescent badger carcasses,
that throb beneath a living, thriving
hive of maggots?

Or feeding the fish
with sacks full of pathetic puppies,
wriggling their way towards the river bed?

Having pregnant fallow hinds gutted,
and turned into red deer
by a pack of lurchers in the black of night,
or white seal pups painted a tainted
shade of scarlet
by the 'humane' men with clubs?

Or making the oceans blush,
bloody furiously,
every time a whale or shoal
of dolphin gets slaughtered?

We even colour the evening sky flame
when we drop napalm to burn
every living thing

on the ground below.

Monochrome Dream

Black skin,
black voice;

song of bloody history.

Black skin,
flogged skin;

a frayed tapestry of oppression.

Black skin,
white teeth;

smile of persecution.

Recalling,
reflecting;

regretting Genesis.

Slaves to yesteryear
and the bigotry of man.

Black beauty?

Black slave?
Black past.

Black skin.
Black Prince.

Black King?

White Queen.
Black Pawn?

Black future?

Rebellious inclination,
bent on the battle;

for respect.

Black face,
black name;
British heart:

still dreaming of freedom.

Fanning the Flames

When the fire snaked across the ceiling
like a heartless dragon, throwing suffocating coils
around the home they still shared, he ran away, his
arms full of sepia photographs and forgotten feelings.

He left his poetry, paintings and his heart, on
a bookshelf in the bedroom, in the burning hope
that if he left the more important things behind, the
flames would ignite the spark they both, once

had known.

Reminiscences

Spinnaker: an extra sail used forward of the mainsail to catch more wind for increased speed

Memory can be a coracle
floating on the mind's ocean,
awash with the salt of tears:

and the sting of surf.

A spinnaker carving shadows
through the sun's hot stare,
gliding out of the past:

like a winged fish out of water.

Cwmaman, Eighty Four

Tory policies killed the mines,
and murdered the Unions with exorbitant fines.

London Police invaded the valleys,
illegally preventing lawful rallies.

With thin grins and fat wage packets,
all shiny buttons and tunic jackets.

"Tony's Tigers" came up from the "Smoke";
a cartoon name but they were no joke.

With "Tony's Tigers" etched and painted
on the bonnets of their Black Marias

the London Met., remain tainted
by this gang of thuggish pariahs,

giving sweets to little girls and boys,
before snatching back these edible toys.

Babies cried whilst the coppers mocked
the valley miners looked on, shocked.

The "Tigers" boasted about their overtime pay;
trying to buy miners' wives sexual play.

When the husbands leapt to their defence,
that was treated as a serious offence.

This was seen as excuse enough;
for "Tony's Tigers" to cut up rough.

They beat the poor lads senseless,
before dragging them off to sentence.

Travesties of justice under a feline pennant,
and the unseeing eyes of their Watch Lieutenant.

There is an inherent flaw,
in the Rule of Law.

When the lawmen, I stress; are themselves lawless.

NOTE: "Tony's Tigers" was not etched and painted on the Black Marias, but were cellophane stickers on the windshields and side windows of the vans. "Tony's Tigers" pennants were flying off the van aerials. All other statements in this poem concerning the London Metropolitan Police's behaviour are true descriptions of actual events – except "giving sweets to...these edible toys". What actually happened was, the policemen offered packets of sweets to the children held in their mother's arms, just out of reach of their little outstretched hands, proceeding to tip the sweets onto the floor where they were ground into the dirt by uniformed boots.

A Blind Man's Colourless Tears

A gentle blush or loving glance cannot be heard
nor seen.

Light and shadow are confused
by his tactile brush

and blurred onto canvas
by caressing fingers,

colour and shape are overdrawn
by opaque eyes.

Her beauty remains undefined
by his deprivation.

His grief stumbles through night –

degraded by darkness.

Ten Years of Tower

- *Archeopterix is a fossil that clearly exhibits characteristics of both dinosaur and bird*
- *Mandril: a small pick used underground*

Raise a glass to Tyrone and the boys, for showing
steel to the Iron Lady.

Raise a glass to Tyrone and the boys, they
looked into the future and saw a mandril was
not an archeopterix, beak down in clay trying
to escape the sound

of pits closing.

Raise a glass to Tyrone and the boys, for knowing
their hands were its wings and although featherless

could still fly.

A Village Lost

As my sad gaze takes in the gutted community,
the Coal Board had abandoned with such alacrity,
I remember the winding wheels of the old pit head,
lifting and lowering colliers, now long dead,
to tear black gold out of rich Welsh soil,
their lungs and bodies broken with honest toil.

Blue scar-mapped bodies still standing proud
from coal face battles won underground.
But although they fought with all their might,
they were quite helpless against the Tory blight.

What chance had they to win the day?

Since Thatcher rigged the law of the land,
so that she could steal the upper hand.

As I cast my eyes forlornly
on fields once grazed by the Welsh pit pony,
I see all that's left after the Conservative's pillage
Is the hopeless plight of a work starved village.

A Collier's Early Retirement

Blue lips wrapped round a racking cough. Coal black
blood spat neatly into a carefully folded handkerchief.
Opaque eyes hide the ache of shadowed lungs.

Pit-propped upright with deathly white pillows. The
silence suffocated by a musical lament of strangled
breaths.

He slumps,
one hand loosely holding the oxygen mask;
the other:

clinging tight to life.

Post Mortem

The mountain
haemorrhaged liquid coal.

And Aberfan bled to death.

A rapid black cancer spread
through the school.

Killing the future.

The tumour should have been treated
and the malignant tissue taken away
before it burst:

and buried a generation.

Eden's Kiss

For Sylvia

The moon serenades mountain and sea as the sun
balances tenderly on the horizon.

The last rays of warm air, tickle lightly – fingers
caressing skin. Voices dance, echoes
of a melliferous tongue and we hear the silent
dragonfly;

flickering wing-beats light as lepidoptera dust.

We embrace wild fruit, its ripe seed nestled in flesh,
fitting the cupped hand like succulent spring-water.

It is time to caress the sky's sensitive lip, kiss the
startled eyes of stars gently winking at the ocean – and
in this enchanted stillness my love

I wish you:

peace on earth and time for the languid moon's liquid
smooth embrace – sweet as fresh drizzled honey, health
enough to wake once more, in love;

and naked in the garden, for if my hands were
continents they still could not hold

the essence of you.

Sleep Walking

For Dad

My father's walk was long and lingering;

yet when I was young,
I slept deeply;
deep enough to touch infinity.

Deep enough to reach pit bottom.

Now; sleeping lightly:
I dream of Maerdy mountain,
and wind ravaged ferns.

I dream of children playing,
among pit props piled high;
beside Cwmaman's overflowing coal trucks.

Where gravel voiced grasshoppers rasped;
beneath scimitar winged swallows,
cutting and thrusting away at halcyon days.

Drams laden with sunlit dreams.

Yet my father's walk was cold and dark,

down that long primeval road,
to the coal rich seams.

My father walked in fossil forests.

Crawled through fossil leaves,
picking at fossil flowers.

Hearing underground streams
fill with silt;

and his lungs with dust.

Infra Red War Cry

Baghdad an oasis of thorns, as smart bombs drop
to crumple uniforms of friend as well as foe
and small arms stick out:

little crosses of collateral.

Are we a pack of wolves
$centing the rich spoor of oil
or Jesus on the Mount
sharing a loaf among a multitude

of Islamic mouths?

As beasts of burden get swamped
in oil-black-body-bags
I clutch at straws from the camel's back

broken by the weight of truth

and the desert's cratered dunes
wears heavy-hearted battle stains
as I peer through army issue night-glasses:

at the resurrected radiance of our sins.

AK's/Aches

Eyes staring dead ahead, ancient AK safely cradled
in crook of elbow

young baby slung from shoulders, both worn casually
like comfortable boots

marching towards the molten stuttering

of enemy arms.

In the aftermath of anarchy, mother and child
cradled gently

in friendly arms

dead eyes staring.

Possession

Pitiless as the sun's hot brand,
two hundred decades of hatred;
blister desert sands.

Old centuries,
sear new misery;
in scorched souls.

The torn tongue,
of sacred doctrine;
splits asunder eastern hearts.

They kneel in nightmares,
candles incandescent;
in each intimate creed.

When darkness descends,
ghosts wail on walls;
I sense the Beast:

in an oasis of thorns.

Body of Christianity

My head; a book of prayer,
read for the fallen children of Iraq.

My heart; a tombstone in a graveyard of living bone,
resurrecting epitaphs, for innocent blood spilt on
the hallowed parchment of:

my skin.

My loins; a lullaby soothing gentile seed:

crucified with grief.

My soul; a brand new Testament etched with shrapnel
from this desert's gritty wound.

The stigmata on my hands and feet:

sluiced away by the crude oil I crawl through.

Cross of Kosovo

In Church,
I prayed on my knees;
until they ached:

an echo of heartfelt pain.

When I rose,
I saw through His glass image;

and it stained my Faith.

Having bitten the broken biscuit and

swallowed Hallowed wine,
I devoured Christianity,
Leaving the bloody bones;

of the fleshless religion:

that abandoned them.

Blasphemy

How can He speak of love,
when every time He opens His mouth,
The word God betrays His voice?

Jesus wept buckets of blood.
Crocodile tears over the dead,
the diseased, the maimed and the starving.

Go to the war stricken little children
with bloated bellies and broken bodies.

for sure as Christ they can't come to you.

Oranges and Lemons

The bridge of truth stood traumatized,
shaken from side to side;
as the March hare tried to reason:

with the abstract march of time.

Truth is often distant,
truth isn't often told;
watch the wrath of orange:

squeeze the lemon cold.

To the haphazard ticking,
of Heath Robinson bombs;
ask the cruel juice of truth:

what you really want to know.

Cold Snap

After the flared breath of dark light,
tides ebb from the shores of morality.

We are the winter.
Black rain deadfall,
meld to the sea.

Frosted survivors,
born of Holocaust;
twisted to hot sand.

A splintered mirror of 'heroic' conflict.

Malformed and translucent,
glaze pitted with reflected atoms;
frozen and cadaverous.

Our charred bones,
frightened white;
hang from broken promises:

brittle as ice.

Sabre Dance

"Little Boy" and "Fat Man" were code/pet names for the two atomic bombs used in World War II

Fission,
the birth and breath of doom;
a dark jitterbug:

split wide open.

The caul of white light,
a glowing lacquer;
liquefies life:

solidifies powder shadows dancing in the womb.

"Little Boy" on Hiroshima,
"Fat Man" on Nagasaki;
flash-bang, flash-bang:

the razzmatazz of radiation.

A cha cha char of marrow-fat,
a jiving twisting fandango;
of tango-ed nerves:

a flamenco of flayed flesh.

"Dem bones,
dem bones;
dem dry bones":

a billion death rattles wrenched from x-rayed throats.

Dark Light

Splintered shadows,
cloak the mushroom sun;
with a massacre:

of aching emptiness

Bleached bones,
peacock bright;
flicker luminously:

in the dark light.

Isotopia

Rainbow-like
a poem in the sky
the radiant lustre;
unexpected –

a pregnant nun.

A Mantra for the Second Millennium

In the beginning:

dark to light.

Rivers of red-hot rock.

Blood:
bubbling from the earth's heart.

Out of magma;
the steam of life.

Then came the cooling:

the blossoming of living cells.

From amoeba, to dinosaur;
and modern man.

From dirt and rock;
to concrete:

burrows and caves;
to skyscrapers.

The future, faster than telepathy;
even more light.

Rocks will boil.

A bright utter radiance:
then the dark.

The history of evolution –

Soil to silo.

The Windows of the World are Covered in Rain

Listen,
to the acid rain;

in test-tube tears.

Lip-read,
silent sounds;
loud with dead.

Then look,
with your microscope's eye;

to measure the fungal shaped stench:

of utter light.

If my sand glazed image,
appears mirrored;
in your scientist's soul?

Reflect:

on the depth of hope.

If the birring clouds,
should cause you doubt?

Have the courage,
to cry,
in the shadow of a gelid sun

lest you hear the fearful smile;

of autumn leaves:

beckon winter.

Progress

Imago and split atom imagery;
the magma of infinity.

Obsolete bombs are fireflies to the sun.

Breath moist with heavy water,
"Fat Man" heads
strain toward heaven.

The miracle of life
can only clutch
at hollow cores;

critical compressed.

They rebut the butterfly's metamorphosis,
yet evoke this charred chrysalis:

as evolution.

Dust delicate, burnt umber wings;
flutter, in the utter light:

hypnotic as they flare.

Picture the next World War
grin, and all the photographs;

are death masks.

Dancers

I wake
writhing in anticipation
of a nuclear black sun.

Where we dance
white boned on atomic ash
wasted, empty of oaths.

A culled chorus-line
twitching
to radiant music

the shadows of our feet
shattered, choreography

contaminated.

River Reverie

Becks and brooks,
fly rods and hooks.

Rocks, pebbles
white water bubbles.

Rivers, streams,
fishermen's dreams.

Golden wish,
silver scaled fish.

Aristocrat

The cuckoo's hyphenated call,
light as lepidoptera dust
floats through air

a double-barrelled note,

that heralds spring – and sibling murder.

Haiku

When the sun
falls into the moon's black hole,
must we all follow?

Jay

The jay's imperial call, rings through deciduous woods,
commanding the trees to welcome him with open arms.

Unfurled leaves ripple like flags waving their allegiance,
whilst branches offer loyalty and devotion, they bend
and dip, as if each perch, as he alights, is bowing to
his Regal Majesty.

With his blue crowned head and blue murder in his heart,
does blue blood run through his veins?

Is he really a King and this emerald canopy:

the jewel in his Realm?

Blue Tits

Chattering sunshine,
glancing through;
the hedgerows:

bright as eyesight.

First Recollection of Blue Tits

As a young child I loved the snow and in winter, as soon
as I awoke, had my nose pressed against the bedroom
window just in case the magic white carpet had flown in
overnight.

For a while I believed blue tits delivered milk in December.

Road-kill

A rattle of dry feathers – a drum roll that states I am
crow, a black quill cloak, with awkward walk and
awkward croak a clarion call

to all that feasts on carrion.

Omen

I am albatross, wings over water, I circumnavigate
oceans on the slightest sigh of air, I sail the surf – and
sight of my silent shadow makes the strongest

seamen shudder.

The Fall

for Tony

I was safe scrumping
hidden in foliage when
Mr Bowen
chased Tony Clarkson out
of the orchard

then the tree shed me:

like an autumn apple.

A Thousand Eyes

A courting peacock
struts a pageant

round his feather crowned head.

Every silky
sun-kissed eye, winking

at the slinky hen.

Swallows

Red white and blue beads
strung along telephone wires
counting summer down

a union jack coloured abacus.

Beached

This poem comes from a photograph of a beached whale in a local paper, Lloret de Mar, Spain 2001 after swimming with pilot whales in Tenerife, Canary Islands one year earlier.

Waters break
and the song of the whale
is miscarried.

Death drowns all music.

The echoing
depth of silence
sounds deafening.

Peregrine

Arrowed,
on a quiver of plumed air;

long flighted:

strong sighted.

Glaring,
flaring;

glowering and staring.

Heavy-browed,
uncowed;

unhooded: hedonistic.

The falcon stoops:

a fletch,

of flint sharp talons.

Eagle

"Shortwing" – a hawk or eagle. Falcons are known as "longwings",
all are falconer's terms. Raptor describes any bird of prey.

Perched,
quarry high,
I watch hawk-eyed through binoculars,
as the regal short-wing quarters the glen,
golden crown ablaze with sun – hunger sharp gaze;

moon cool.

She soars the sky on broad sails that billow,
on pillows of warm wind,

until,

wings spill buoyant air
and she spears cloud,
becomes lethal as smoke;

the raptor drops in haloes of deceit,
closing on her quarry faster than a forest fire,
to pounce the last few feet:

rapier thrusts of legs and claymore claws,
flash at highland hare.

After the kill:

flame shaped wings,
spiral away on thermals of hot air.

Tawny Owl

In nature's cathedral,
where blue bells chime;
and snowdrops bow their heads;

as if in prayer.

At night,
quiet as a church mouse;
a cryptic coloured predator:

preys –

swooping through wooded aisles,
on wings;
silent as the 'p':

in psalm.

Mine-Field

At fly-blown nipples
of barren breasts

the lips
of bomb shattered babies
suck
at the milk of human kindness

The death masks of taut skin
a world-wide tattoo of condemnation

drummed into oblivion.

Good Friday Agreement

Even as mountain whins shiver, to the shatter of
distant drums.

Stilled trigger fingers, rifle through the dead,
healing the septic sting of gunfire;
cleansing the metallic stain of conflict:

sweeping over the bloodshed like the laying on of
hands.

Sharp tongued gorse,
wreathed in prayer;
flower monumentally:

for the victims of a hundred hurtful years.

Bright yellow petals that grieve for all the suffering,
hint a golden lustre of resurrection.

A Christmas Carol

After Seamus Heaney's 'Puma'

God put the vixen in the valleys to conduct the chapels'
high choirs. Her screams overhang the South Wales pits
like snow on granite quarries – as if her song, was
somehow

Deep-mined.

She haunts the blizzard's howl with her acoustics. Her
music
soars the shattered air. A siren of the setts – all night
she sings to Heaven with a hymn like shrapnel, whilst
the moon

orchestrates her psalms.

Afterwards, in daylight, she lies in her white form,
worn out

like a prayer.

*Form – A snug place to rest made new each time by the animal
turning round in circles, whether in grass or snow, until
comfortable and used when it is above ground and too far away
from its underground home.*

*Sett – A series of connecting tunnels and chambers dug in the
hillside, normally on the edge of woods or forests, by generations
of badgers. Foxes usually use old, deserted setts but occasionally
will share a badger's home.*

Hobby

Red thigh booted falcon
strutting the sky
out-flying prey, swallow and dragonfly.

Stage-Struck

The dark curtains,
a shroud for all tomorrows;
unfurl their horror to sightless eyes:

greeting blind stupidity with thunderous applause.

The last night has come,
ungratefully.

Smothering invincibility,
with billowing pillows of holocaust.

The audience wither:

utterly stage-struck.

Wild Horses

I dream of horses
stampeding
galloping after hot breath.

Instead pit ponies
bred to sweat
haunt nightmares darkly shackled

Blind to light
fields summertime fresh
sad with herds.

Bee-Eaters

Turquoise bodies and noiseless wings poised
to follow the swallowed sun:

burning through their throats.

Rattle snake

Silk lanyard loosely wound
in a wither of grass.

Jacob's Organ
jangling a tongue of tang.

Sleeveless skin
of sly ambush.

A venomous whip of speed
rattling to slough a shadow

at a jitter of nerves.

Viper

A mosaic of black and white
a crinkled coil of warmed serenity
a scaled, silent secret

hidden in bright sunlight.

Queen of the Valleys

Ruled out
  Slumped.
  Sumptuous green robes ripped wide open,
  raped of her mineral wealth.
  Black diamond pyramids laid flat and fallow,
  pit-head machinery split and pitted,
  rusted, iron-boned towers lowered,
  winding wheels wound down,
  flawed government schemes,
  shattered dreams.
  Dead economy.

Dole for coal
  Dumped.
  Proud, blue-scarred men no longer credit-worthy.
  Crushed mines, crushed miners.
  Unemployment rife,
  devastated towns, devastated life.
  Zinc sheeted pubs and shops
  with plywood windows;
  a bleak, desolate, post-industrial landscape,
  killing expectation.

Generations degenerate here
  Pumped
  Bingo halls, clubs and takeaways.
  Vomit on the pavement and piss on the walls.
  I sit in a decrepit old youth club,
  watching bodies full of spirits

and heads full of emptiness
Twitch and jerk,
out of rhythm, out of rhyme,
out of tempo, out of time.
Children choked on dope
or whiskey, or tv soap,
devoid of hope.
Sniff the glue.
Blank, vacant,
vacuous, void.

Wasted
Stumped.
Grievous for fun.
No escape.
Now or ever.
Sit and scrounge.
Dead souls loiter under a coal black cloud.
Boredom. Despair.
Fucked
Trumped.
Failed.
Nailed.
Jailed.

Noble collier footprints fade away.

Angling

For Darren
Redds – spawning grounds; Wooden Priest – a cudgel to kill fish

A country bridge
over gravel beds.

Hazy heat,
a languid river.

Skimming swallows
and salmon redds.

Sun-kissed promises
from an Indian giver.

Dry fly,
leaping sewin.

Lush green meadow,
lazy shallows.

Clear blue sky,
buzzards mewing.

Game fish caught
On a split cane gallows.

Finally,
eyes lowered to the feast.

Grace given
by a wooden priest.

Salmo Salvar

For Darren

Amidst the reed beds
of this estuary
I tremble, nursing

the bruised net of my coracle.

Is this the voice of Salmo, a reverberation
of your soul?

With legs spread to each front corner
fingers, sculled around the tide

I sail the dorsal fins of salmon

angling for the quiet echo:

of your voice.

Ghost

For Darren

Mist forms shadows on the Teifi. I walk through their
opaqueness. I need a breeze to refresh memory, a storm
to drown regret, a promise of anticipation

and a vow not to break the translucence.

If you stroll all day through woods you will not find a
birch tree worth a canoe
but hazel can be coppiced,
collected, split and knit into a coracle
if only you'd trust your hide

to my hands.

I taught you to read owl pellets, pupae, butterfly wings
and spider silk spun and hung on fern. To follow badger
spoor spotted with berry seed, battle through nettles and
not care if bare legs are stung. We have walked the
Pembrokeshire coastal path from Poppit to Amroth,
swallowed all edible fungi and allowed the snake to scent
our path with tongue and Jacob's Organ yet you never
taught me the exhilaration of white water, the calm of
deep pools or the craft to find and tail big salmon.

I want to remember dawn so I wait for a falcon's stoop,
a dove to flutter its wings or an otter to break

the electric stillness.

At Rest

His stiff embrace, as if
embarrassed

blushed between my arms
like an awkward silence

coldbruised and screaming

unlike the warmhug of night silence
at the river bank

where I still sit to soak up
his poacher's pocket

of peace.

Dedicated to our son, Darren Troy Morrissey, 18th August 1970 – 27th August 1994. An artist, naturalist, poet and singer/songwriter.